oh how I love snow.
oh how I love snow.
MW01078490

The Book of Gifts

LUCY CLAIRE DUNBAR

The Book of Gifts

LUCY CLAIRE DUNBAR

For all those that helped me through,
every single one of you, I hope you know
you never walk alone.

X

Hello, you lovely soul,

If you're reading this, I think you are meant to be here. I am a firm believer in trusting the universe – the good, the bad, the sunshine, the showers – they are put in our path to guide us.

My twenty-seven years on this earth have been a roller-coaster and, having danced with death more times than I ever thought possible, it is a miracle I am here. My gosh, has it made me feel lucky to be alive and blessed to have you here, and I hope that everything I have been through will help another soul in a time of need. I never thought I would do much with my life, a lost cause, but I am slowly realizing my purpose all along was just to be me – we are enough just as we are.

I hope this book can remind us of the gifts of life. However hard our days can be, there is always hope of a brighter tomorrow and, most importantly, the knowledge that everything you need to get through is inside. You have had the strength in you all along.

If I can help one person with these sketches, I have achieved more in my life than I ever thought possible.

This book has been a journey and, if I am honest, I don't know how we got here – a lot of wrong turns, dead ends and what felt like endless roundabouts, but I realize more and more that that's just life. There is no right way or wrong way, only your way.

For a lot of my life, I struggled in the dark, afraid I wasn't worthy of happiness. Afraid there wasn't anything left in me to fight. It is only once we surface and see the first glimmers that we realize those were our strongest hours.

To love is one of life's greatest gifts. We hope that our first and last breaths are surrounded by it, and our lives are full of it, as without it we would simply cease to be. It's the warmth of a smile, the melody of a laugh, the beat of a heart. In my opinion, it's love that makes the world go round and it's love thats got us this far.

THE GIFT OF

Love can heal a broken heart, mend a worn-down soul, give hope when all is lost.

Love is magic, love is hope, love is sometimes all we've got.

The answer is always LOVE

Sometimes letting go

is the most loving

thing to do.

create the world you dream of.

Something worth searching for.

The Brighter Times
We are all human.
We are all trying
our best.
We all deserve a
moment to rest,
with time, love and
respect.

Reminder:
you give so much love, don't forget to save some for you
x

When you feel like giving up on yourself,
please know the world hasn't given up on you.

YOU CARRIED
ON AND THAT'S
AS BRAVE AS
IT COMES

It's the little moments
that mean the most.

Love has no
rhyme nor reason,
just a beautiful
feeling.

The grass is greener

where you water it.

With love in our hearts and friends by our side, everything else is the cherry on top of a beautiful life.

Now. Then. Forever. Always.

When you listen to
your heart, happiness
is never truly far.

Friendship. Where do I start!

Friendship is quite literally that, the ship

that pulls us through our darkest hour,

and weathers every storm.

THE GIFT OF *friendship*

N
E
S
W

Friendship is the journey we hope will last forever, no matter where it takes us.

We can't stop the storms, but we will make it through. We always do.

friendship

True friends show you the light when you're struggling in the dark.

Sometimes in life,

I can't find the right words,

but know

in my heart

you'll always be heard.

It's okay to ask for help sometimes.

We'll be here through the storms,
through it all, till you find the sunshine.

Sometimes it's not about seeing the magic,

but knowing it's there.

Friendship is the beat inside your heart
that keeps us moving on.

True friends are like stars.

You can't always see them,

but they are always there.

Home isn't a place, it's a feeling.

Sometimes 'I've got you' is all

we need to hear

to know we'll be okay.

Maybe your purpose was to be you all along.

True friendship is comfort in the silence.

Gratitude is the gift that keeps on giving.
When we realize each day isn't a given,
that each dawn is truly the present, well,
I think that's winning life's jackpot.
I hope these sketches can be a little
reminder that happiness is never truly
far away with love in our hearts.

THE GIFT OF *gratitude*

September
Today
is the miracle, everything
else is pure magic.

The greatest gift is time with you.

capture every moment - one day these
magic photos will be our greatest treasure.

Make time for the little moments.

The future will be brilliant, but for now lets just focus on the present.

NOW
NOW
NOW
NOW
NOW
NOW
NOW
NOW
NOW
NOW
NOW
NOW

You can't control the cards you're dealt,

just learn to play the hand.

Maybe the amount of
EXTRAORDINARY
things that happen
in your life
DEPENDS ON
what you
NOTICE.

When we realize that life

is the winning ticket,

the real jackpot is won.

You're exactly where you're supposed to be.

It's Okay to
SLOW Down.
GOOD THings
take Time.

And then one day life feels brighter, lighter.

Today

Don't let the worry of tomorrow
make you miss out on the gift of today.

When we are small, we believe courage to be bold, fierce and loud. But courage can be as simple as waking up, putting your best foot forward and carrying on. I hope you know how brave you've been, and that the strength you need to carry on was in you all along.

THE GIFT OF *courage*

It takes courage to take on the world every day.

You are brighter than your
darkest thought
and stronger than your
greatest fear.

Without the darkest
of times,
we would never
have met the stars.

Love is the
greatest mark
we can leave in
our path.

courage

You've made it through the darkest of storms, keep going.

Sometimes courage is taking the leap
into the unknown.

A world where children
can dare to dream
is a place I'd like to be.

Maybe it feels like

because it is.

I hope when you look back you'll see how far you've come, all the silent battles that you've won.

The strength you have within is greater than you'd ever think.

Bravery is facing the world when battling your own storm.

courage

I don't know if we truly understand love until we have lost a loved one. It is the reminder we need to share as much as possible, treasure the time we have for all that it is, and love as deeply as our hearts allow. One thing I have learnt about grief is that it never fades, only changes. I hope you know their love will always be there.

Near or far, forever in your heart.

THE GIFT OF

All that I am,

you taught me to be.

If heaven had a phone, I'd call you just to say,

I love you, I miss you, each and every day.

Near or far, forever in our hearts.

To have one more moment with you.

We may be just a blip in time, but the love we leave behind will always shine.

memories

I still see you in the beauty of every day.

Robins appear when loved ones are near.

All it takes is a single feather to know you're there.

Music holds a thousand stories old and young, songs still left unsung.

I miss you in
the little moments.

If you were snow, I'd wait out in a thousand storms for one more moment with you.

Kindness is the greatest superpower any of us possesses. It is knowing the light you give will help someone glow. It is helping a stranger in need find their feet. It is giving without expecting in return. I believe kindness can change the world. I know the smallest act of kindness can truly save a life.

THE GIFT OF *kindness*

I believe kindness can save the world.

I know kindness can save a life.

Kind words plant seeds of hope.

Be the light you needed
on your darkest day.

Kindness Cafe

CHECK OUT

a smile	£0.00
words of encouragement	£0.00
patience	£0.00
time for a loved one	£0.00
being gentle with yourself	£0.00
Grand Total	£0.00

Small acts of kindness

lead to great blooms of hope.

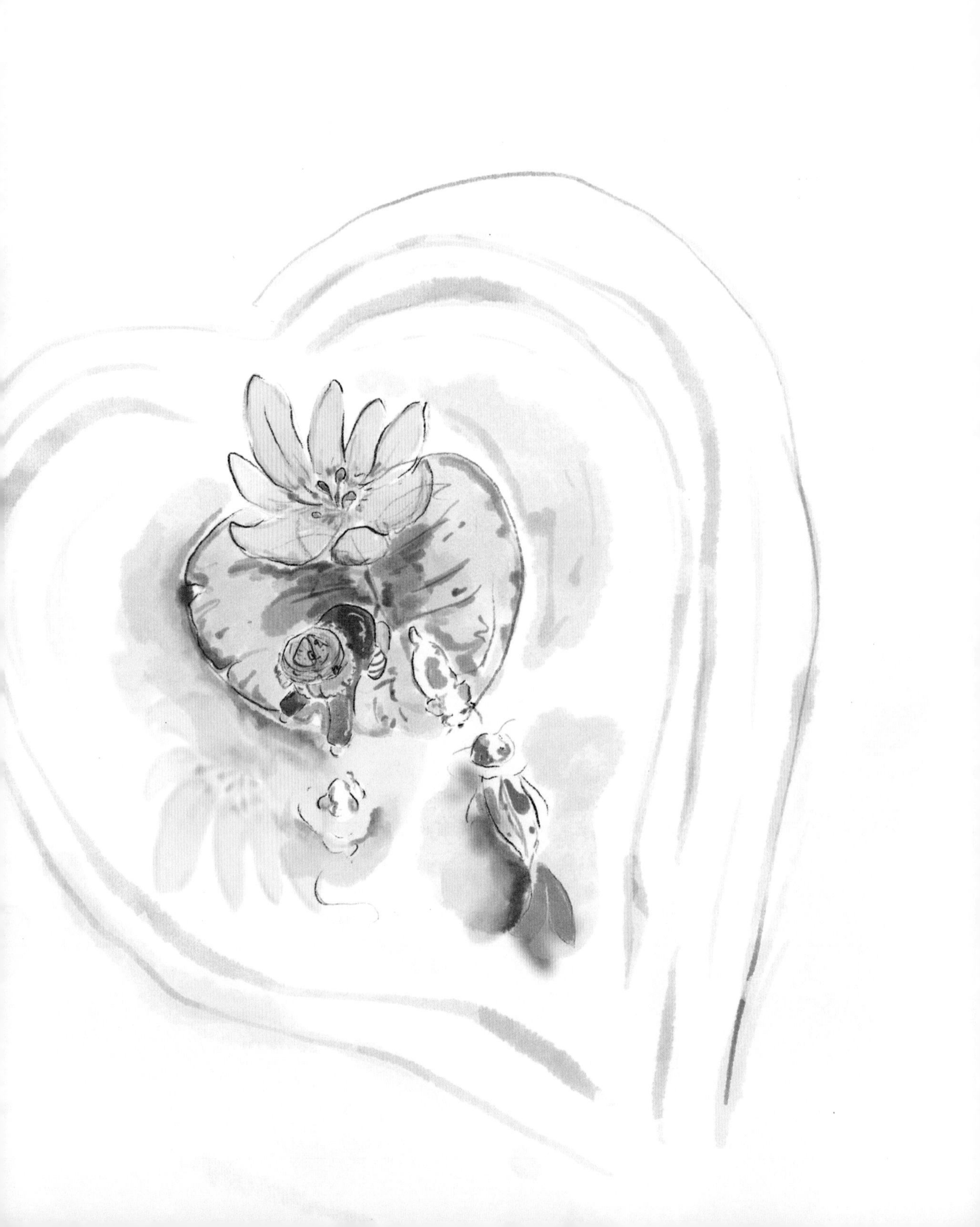

The tiniest act of kindness

can cause the greatest wave of love.

You aren't a
burden, you're
just healing.

Just like the tides,
life ebbs and flows.
Sometimes it's okay
to just stay afloat.

For a lot of my life, I thought I was broken, I couldn't figure out why I didn't seem to 'work' like my brothers and sisters. It's only now I realize I was doing what I needed to survive. That's all we can do. I know now there is no right way to survive, you do what you need to do to get through. So go easy on yourself, take care of yourself and most importantly, forgive yourself.

THE GIFT OF
Self-love

36
REST
The best medicine
for healing hearts
and souls
for when your brain's a
mess, you've lost your way,
and just need a little TLC.

You aren't
broken,
just human.

We all need to take it slow sometimes.

you don't need to be fixed, just loved.

The world is your oyster,

but for now it's okay to rest.

Tomorrow is a new day,

a blank canvas to start again.

You are worthy.

Sometimes hitting pause

is the self-love you deserve.

you made it
through
and that is
ENOUGH.

do what
you can
today.

It's your story to make.

to rewrite the ending.

You are
loved

Sometimes the
Most productive
thing to do is
REST.

Take what you need.

We all need a little extra love sometimes, go easy on yourself.

Be a flamingo in a flock full of pigeons.

One day you'll realize being you

was enough all along.

Some days good enough really is enough.
Rest

YOUR THOUGHTS
ARE NOT
YOUR TRUTH.

Give Yourself
PERMISSION
to
Rest.

We all need to switch off sometimes.

Don't miss the moon,

whilst trying to catch the stars.

self-love

Dance to the beat

of your own drum.

My ducks are absolutely not in a row.

I don't even know where some of them are,

and I'm pretty sure one of them is a pigeon.

You don't need a thicker skin.

Even broken crayons bring so much beauty to the world.

The greatest achievements

start with a dream.

Reminder:
you give
so much
love, save
some for
you
x

You are worthy
of happiness, of time, most importantly love
Every storm has its dawn,
HAPPY DAYS
GOOD NEWS
gazette
BREAKING NEWS
You are
Enough
just as you are
always have been, always will be

There is no race when you're

going at your own pace.

In a world where you can be anything,

BE YOU.

You can't be everyone's cup of tea,

and that's okay.

There is no greater perfection than being true to your heart.

If we expected a plant to bloom straight away,

we would miss the joy of watching it grow.

I like staying in and finding peace within.

There's so much joy ahead, I hope you take a moment to be proud of how far you've come.

I put my heart on paper so that, if tomorrow I wake up and the world has gone dark again, I'll know I drew everything I could. I guess writing this book is the dream I thought was gone, the fact I will be able to see the drawings I've created in a book. Well, its about as full circle as it gets.

If anything comes from this book, I hope it helps someone somewhere whose world has gone dark, who can't see a way through. I've been there, each day feels like a marathon. One day at a time, and suddenly you realize life is brighter, life is lighter. You made it through the storm.

THE GIFT OF

In my darkest hours, hope was all I had. At twenty-one I lost my sight; my world quite literally went dark. No longer able to read, my friends would help me sign my forms for uni, I couldn't even cross the road by myself. Gosh, looking back I don't know how I survived. Hope of a brighter tomorrow was all I had to pull me through. I am blessed to say – with help – I had most of my vision restored and, my word, am I grateful for it every day. This is why I draw so much; when I lay my head to rest at night, I want to know I have drawn the gifts the day has shown me.

Behind the darkest of storms,

there is always light.

When it feels like all is lost . . .

sometimes hope is all we've got.

Hope is the light that guides us home.

Even in the darkest of times there is hope.

May the moon remind us, even in the darkest of times, we are enough, just as we are.

Tomorrow
Will be Brighter
just hold
Tight
x

Sometimes we just need a reminder that the darkness won't last forever. That's the thing about storms. We can't always stop them coming, but they will always pass.

May you never forget, even after
the darkest of chapters, there are
brighter days to come.

Spring is the sign from nature
that it will all be okay.

Spring is nature's final melody

before summer's grand crescendo.

Hope is to believe in a brighter tomorrow.

that lifts us up.

you Made
it
THrougH

May the sun be your reminder
there are brighter days to come.

Even the darkest of nights

has its dawn.

Penguin Michael Joseph

UK | USA | Canada | Ireland | Australia
India | New Zealand | South Africa

Penguin Michael Joseph, Penguin Random House UK,
One Embassy Gardens, 8 Viaduct Gardens, London SW11 7BW

penguin.co.uk
global.penguinrandomhouse.com

First published 2024
003

Design by Penguin Dan

Set in Sage & Pink
Colour reproduction by Altaimage Ltd
Printed and bound in Great Britain by Bell & Bain Ltd, Glasgow

The authorized representative in the EEA is Penguin Random House Ireland,
Morrison Chambers, 32 Nassau Street, Dublin D02 YH68

A CIP catalogue record for this book is available from the British Library

ISBN: 978-0-241-71917-6

www.greenpenguin.co.uk

Penguin Random House is committed to a sustainable future for our business, our readers and our planet. This book is made from Forest Stewardship Council® certified paper.